Get Stronger!

Written by Maryann Dobeck

CELEBRATION PRESS

Pearson Learning Group

Do you want to get stronger?
Run like a horse!

Do you want to get stronger?
Climb like a monkey!

Do you want to get stronger?
Swim like a fish!

Do you want to get stronger?
Hop like a frog!

Do you want to get stronger?
Lift like an elephant!

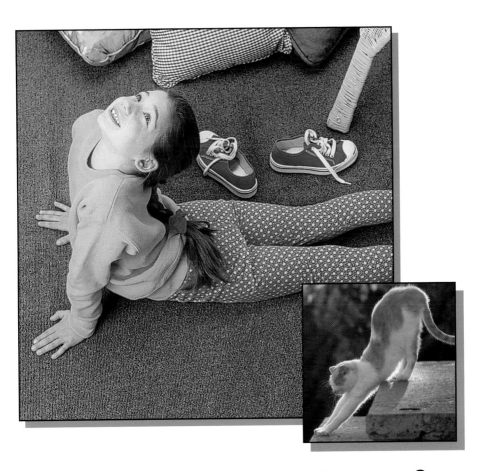

Do you want to get stronger?
Stretch like a cat!

Get stronger!
You can do it!